D0962514

A Gift For:

_____

From:

_____

Wit and Wisdom of Disney
© 2012 Disney
Based on the "Winnie the Pooh" works by A.A. Milne and E.H. Shepard.
Based on *The Hundred and One Dalmatians* by Dodie Smith, published by The Viking Press.
Based on the Mowgli Stories in *The Jungle Book* and *The Second Jungle Book* by Rudyard Kipling.
Tim Burton's The Nightmare Before Christmas is based on a story and characters by Tim Burton.

© 2012 Disney/Pixar

2011 Hallmark Licensing, LLC
Published by Hallmark Gift Books,
a division of Hallmark Cards, Inc.,
Kansas City, MO 64141
Visit us on the Web at Hallmark.com.

Editor: Emily Osborn
Art Director: Kevin Swanson
Designer and Production Artist: Dan Horton
Art & Design Development: Madeline Tompkins

ISBN: 978-1-59530-297-7

BOK3107

Printed and bound in China

Wit and
Wisdom of
Disney

TABLE OF CONTENTS

Introduction

Walt Disney (1901–1966) was one of the most legendary icons and innovators in history. Creator and original voice of the beloved Mickey Mouse, Disney received 59 Academy Award nominations and won seven Emmy Awards and 26 Oscars, including four in one year, giving him more awards and nominations than any other individual.

Wit and Wisdom of Disney is a compilation of some of Disney's most wise and witty, memorable and inspirational quotes—from both the man himself and your favorite cast of characters—on the subjects of friendship, love, life's little quirks, dreams and aspirations, and being yourself.

"If you can *dream* it, you can *do* it."

–Walt Disney

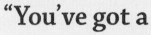

"You've got a

friend in *me*."

–Randy Newman, *Toy Story*

Finding Friendship

"The nice thing about
friends,"
said Pooh,

"is that they are so
very friendly."

–Winnie the Pooh

"Nothing is more important than our friendship."

–Sulley, *Monsters, Inc.*

"Everybody knows a dog's **best friend** is his human."

–Lady and the Tramp

"I'm happier than a **tornado** in a **trailer park.**"

–Mater, *Cars*

"It's good to keep your friends within hugging distance."

–Pooh & Tigger, *Winnie the Pooh*

"If Bolt's taught me **anything,** it's that you **never** abandon a friend at a **time of need!**"

—Rhino, *Bolt*

"Oh, Al.

I'm gettin' **kinda fond** of you,
kid.

Not that I wanna pick out

curtains or anything."

–Genie, *Aladdin*

"There's a great big hunk of world out there

with no fences around it...

and beyond those distant hills,

who knows what wonderful experiences.

And it's all ours for the taking."

—Tramp, *Lady and the Tramp*

"'We'll be *friends forever,*
won't we, Pooh?'

asked Piglet.

Even longer, '
Pooh answered."

– *Winnie the Pooh*

"Faith,
Trust, and
Pixie dust."

—Tinker Bell, *Peter Pan*

"When everything's blustery

and you're feeling flustery,

remember

you have friends

who care."

–*Winnie the Pooh*

"**If you can't say**

something nice...

don't say

nothing at all."

– Thumper, *Bambi*

"Hakuna Matata."

–Timon and Pumba, *The Lion King*

Dealing with Life's
Little Quirks

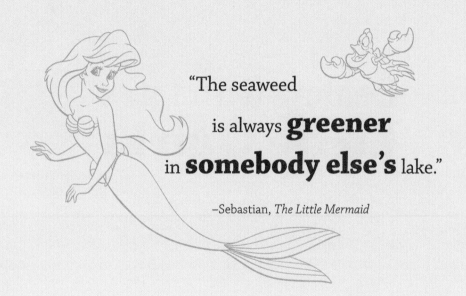

"The seaweed

is always **greener**

in **somebody else's** lake."

–Sebastian, *The Little Mermaid*

"The very things
that held you down
are gonna carry you **up**

and **up**

and **up.**"

–Timothy Mouse, *Dumbo*

"Just
keep
swimming."

–Dory, *Finding Nemo*

"I always like to look
on the **optimistic** side of life,
but I am **realistic** enough to know
that life is a **complex** matter."

–Walt Disney

"Keep your chin up.

Someday there will be

happiness again."

–Robin Hood

"The flower
that *blooms*
in *adversity*
is the most rare
and *beautiful* of all."

—Fa Zhou, Mulan

"You may not realize it when it happens, but **a kick in the teeth** may be the best thing in the world for you."

–Walt Disney

"Things will look better in the morning."

–Bagheera, *The Jungle Book*

"FIND A HAPPY PLACE!
FIND A HAPPY PLACE!
FIND A HAPPY PLACE!"

—Peach, *Finding Nemo*

"We keep *moving* forward,

opening new doors,

and *doing* new things,

because we're curious

and curiosity keeps *leading* us

down new paths."

–Walt Disney

"*No one can order me to stop dreaming.*"

–Cinderella

Following Your Dreams

"Why,

if I picked a day to *fly*,

oh, *this* would *be it*."

–Quasimodo, *The Hunchback of Notre Dame*

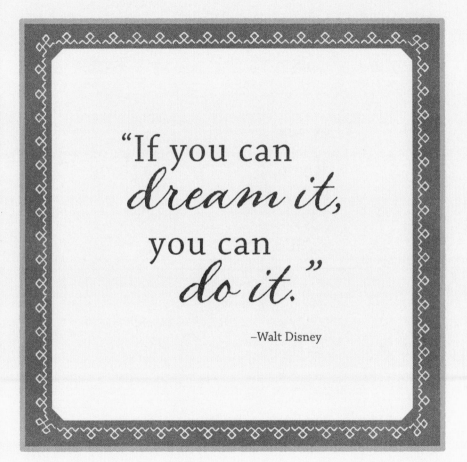

"If you can *dream it,*
you can
do it."

–Walt Disney

"They say
if you *dream* a thing
more than once,
it's sure
to come true."

–Briar Rose, *Sleeping Beauty*

"It's kind of **fun** to do the **impossible.**"

–Walt Disney

"A man has **dreams**
of **walking** with giants.
To **carve** his niche
in the edifice of time."

–George Banks, *Mary Poppins*

"TO INFINITY...AND BEYOND!"

– Buzz Lightyear, *Toy Story*

"When you **believe** in a thing, **believe** in it **all the way, implicitly** and **unquestionably.**"

—Walt Disney

"When you're **footloose** and **collar-free,** well, you take **nothing but the best.**"

—Tramp, *Lady and the Tramp*

"Change is nature.
    The part we can influence.
And it starts
    when we decide."

–Remy, *Ratatouille*

"Nothing's *impossible.*"

–Doorknob, *Alice in Wonderland*

"It's **good** to be **bad**."

–Cruella Deville, *101 Dalmatians*

Being
Yourself

"I walk on the **wild side.**
I **laugh** in the face
of **danger!**"

–Simba, *The Lion King*

"This much I knew.

If you **are** what you eat,

then I **only** wanna eat

the good stuff."

–Remy, *Ratatouille*

"I give myself

very good advice,

but I

seldom follow it."

–Alice, *Alice in Wonderland*

"Oh, it's not the first time
I was tossed out of a window,
and it won't be the last.
What can I say?
I'm a rebel."

–Rudy, *The Emperor's New Groove*

"How sentimental.
You know,
I haven't been this choked up
since I got a hunk of moussaka
caught in my throat."

–Hades, *Hercules*

"The more you like *yourself,* the less you are like *anyone else,* which makes you *unique.*"

–Walt Disney

"Jack, please,
I'm only an
elected official here.
I can't make decisions
by myself!"

–Mayor, *The Nightmare Before Christmas*

"I'm so **happy** I could **bounce!**"

–Tigger, *Winnie the Pooh*

"This is **you.**
This is your **badness** level.
It's **unusually high**
for someone
your size."

–Lilo, *Lilo and Stitch*

"I am a **nice** shark,
not a **mindless** eating machine.
If I am to change this image,
I must first **change myself.**
Fish are **friends,**
not food."

–Bruce, *Finding Nemo*

"*Love* will always *find a way.*"

–Sleeping Beauty

Falling in Love

"My name is Dug.
I have **just met** you,
and I **love** you."

-Dug, Up

"Sometimes the **smallest** things take up the most room **in your heart.**"

-*Winnie the Pooh*

"There is *nowhere* you can go where *love can't follow.*"

– 101 Dalmatians

"Nearly **everybody** gets **twitterpated** in the **springtime.**"

—Friend Owl, *Bambi*

"**Ohana** means **family**;
family means **nobody** gets left behind
or **forgotten**."

–Lilo, *Lilo and Stitch*

"Ladies don't **start** fights,
but they can **finish** them!"

–Marie, *The Aristocats*

"As far as I could see,
the old **notion** that a bachelor's life
was so...
glamorous and **carefree**
was all **nonsense.**
It was **downright dull.**"

—Roger, 101 Dalmatians

"I look at you and I'm home."

–Dory, *Finding Nemo*

"Well, you know how **men** are.

They think **'No'** means **'Yes'**

and **'Get lost'** means

'Take me, I'm yours!'"

—Meg, Hercules

"With every *kiss,*
we'll promise this:
we'll find a way to light the dawn
of all we wish."

—*Pocahontas*

Absence makes the heart
grow fonder...or forgetful.

—Peter Pan

...and they lived

happily ever after.

**If you have enjoyed this book
or it has touched your life in some way,
we would love to hear from you.**

Please send your comments to:

Hallmark Book Feedback
P.O. Box 419034
Mail Drop 215
Kansas City, MO 64141

Or e-mail us at:

booknotes@hallmark.com

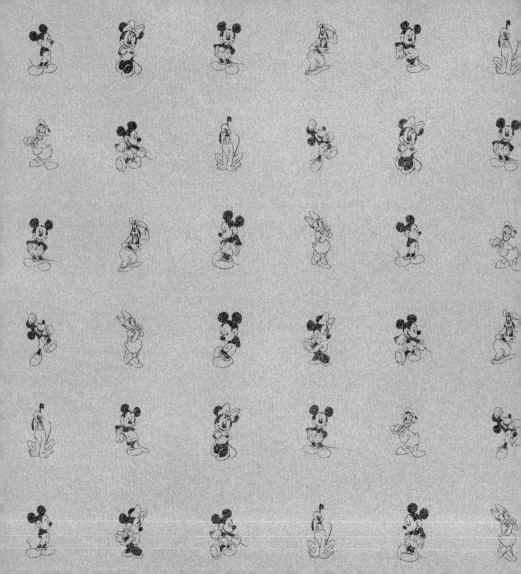